JONATHAN CONALLY

THE GREAT CHOLESTEROL CON

The Essential Guide to TLC Diet Transformation, Learn How the TLC Diet Can Help Lower Your Cholesterol and Lose Weight to Transform Your Life

Descrierea CIP a Bibliotecii Naționale a României
JONATHAN CONALLY
THE GREAT CHOLESTEROL CON. The Essential Guide
to TLC Diet Transformation, Learn How the TLC Diet Can
Help Lower Your Cholesterol and Lose Weight to Transform
Your Life / Jonathan Conally. – Bucharest: Editura My Ebook, 2020
    ISBN

JONATHAN CONALLY

THE GREAT CHOLESTEROL CON

The Essential Guide to TLC Diet Transformation, Learn How the TLC Diet Can Help Lower Your Cholesterol and Lose Weight to Transform Your Life

My Ebook Publishing House
Bucharest, 2020

CONTENTS

INTRODUCTION

Let's start this beginners guide on the TLC diet with a little mental exercise. When you go out, look around you and tell me what you see. I bet you will see an abundance of fast food restaurants and guess what's in front of them? You guessed it…A never-ending line of people.

Fast food joints are known for serving up a dish of unhealthy food - unhealthy food that people continue to consume. Why? Because they can! People choose fast food because they live a busy life and are under the impression that they can't go home and cook a healthy meal, because it will take hours to do.

This unhealthy lifestyle leads to obesity.

The health risks of being obese include:

- Heart disease

- Type 2 diabetes

- Osteoarthritis

- Nonalcoholic fatty liver disease

- High blood pressure

- Stroke

Reasons People Are Unhealthy

- Most work available is white-collar

- Children now spend more time playing digital games instead of playing outside

- The foods low-income families can afford are unhealthy

- The serving sizes of unhealthy drinks have increased

- People buy more fast food and prepare fewer meals in their kitchen

This list could go on and on …

There's an old Chinese proverb that does a good job at explaining why we need to watch what we put in our mouths. "When you're thirsty, it's too late to dig a well." What this is saying is that you should not wait until you have an illness to start a diet, because by then, it may be too late.

The Need For Health In The Modern Age

There are many important reasons as to why you should get in shape today. What "getting in shape" means to me is you have strength, a baseline cardiovascular capacity, muscular endurance and flexibility, which all leads to a healthier life.

Believe it or not, the 21st century conditions could be damaging your health and you don't even realize it. Let's have a look at some of these modern-day health conditions being experienced …

Toasted Skin Syndrome

Have you ever heard of this? Have you ever balanced your laptop on your knees for a long period of time? Believe it or not, It can leave you with discolored skin!

The heat is generated by your laptop, it causes a rash that is similar to someone that has huddled to close to a heater in order to stay warm. Mind you, this has nothing to do with dieting or exercise – this is just showing you how our health is being affected in the modern age by technology.

Time Poverty

Oh yes, good old time poverty – so many of us are a victim of this. With family, work, running a home, and trying to take care of everything, we hardly find time to sit down and pause for a nice breath of fresh air. The more we rush, the further we struggle to meet deadlines we have imposed. The result? Our health. We deal with everything from insomnia, stress, depression and poor diet, which leads to obesity and many other health related issues. Many of us are simply doing too much and in return, this is taking a major toll on our health and well-being.

Living in Fear

Many will refer to this as "the 21st century fear." Here we are, constantly staring at the threat of floods, disease, crime, hurricanes, terrorist attacks, toxic chemicals in food and so much more. We're constantly focusing on those fears. We have become so worried about the things that "might" happen to the point that we have stopped enjoying life that is taking place in front of us.

As you may already know, too much worry isn't good for your health.

We may not be able to help you with toasted skin syndrome, other than tell you not to place your laptop on your lap for a prolonged time, but we may be able to help you with time poverty. This is where the TLC diet is going to come into play.

You see, in the modern day scenario, everything comes at a price. Our days and nights are filled with hectic schedules, unavoidable deadlines and innumerable hours of stress and excessive workload. With so much already on our plate, we cease to care about the food what we consume at the end of a long tiring day.

Most often, we are too tired to cook a healthy, nutritious meal post work and end up opting for the easier option: fast food and processed items. With the blooming technology, everything is just a click or a phone call away.

As we previously stated, most people settle for a comforting double cheese burger, pizza or fries to hush their roaring stomach every day. Although these food choices offer oodles of contentment and comfort, eventually they bring forth drastic side effects. Overtime, with continuous consumption, unhealthy food choices lead to several modern day ailments, such as diabetes, obesity, hypertension, depression, anxiety, high cholesterol and other related concerns.

Most of these complaints start out small but gradually turn into unavoidable chronic conditions. The best idea is to wake up, take action and prevent such ailments from deteriorating your health and fitness further.

For all those facing similar conditions, this short beginners guide brings a suitable solution to combat most of our modern day problems. It introduces the concept of the TLC Diet or the Therapeutic Lifestyle Changes program.

Are you ready? Let's get started...

CHAPTER 1

WHAT EXACTLY IS THE TLC DIET?

This diet focuses mainly on modifying the increasing or already hyped levels of cholesterol.

When the body contains an excessive level of cholesterol, over time it weakens the heart and causes several fatal conditions, like a sudden heart attack and stroke among other serious cardio vascular conditions.

It is highly recommended to take charge of your body and health before it worsens beyond repair.

This diet encourages healthy measures to lower cholesterol levels by means of diet, exercise and other related methods. It also brings successful weight loss in its wake. For all those struggling with weight loss or health conditions, the TLC diet is a great way to kick start your way to good health and wellbeing.

The Therapeutic Lifestyle Changes diet was initially coined by the NATIONAL Heart, lung and blood institute in the year 2001. Due to its beneficial nature, the diet has also been approved and encouraged by the American Heart Association.

The diet aims at reducing the LDL levels of cholesterol, also known as the bad cholesterol, which is held responsible for triggering cardio vascular complications.

The diet focuses mainly on healthy food options that have been coupled with suitable exercise and required lifestyle changes to help speed the process of recovery without any medications.

It not just keeps the LDL levels in control but also works towards providing the body the right level of HDL or the good healthy cholesterol that is required by the body for proper functioning, induced growth and development.

Although the diet does bring about some weight loss in its process, the goal is improved health by controlling cholesterol more than focusing solely on losing weight.

Well that's a quick overview of what the TLC diet is, over the next few chapters we will cover exactly what cholesterol is, the benefits of starting a TLC diet program and what foods you need to include in your everyday diet.

CHAPTER 2

ALL ABOUT CHOLESTEROL

Again, and again, food and diet has been named as the major culprit for causing health problems around the world.

High blood pressure or Hypertension is now a very big problem. It is considered the number one killer in America, and perhaps in many other countries around the world.

Undoubtedly, a person with a high blood pressure is facing many risks in relation to health. There are many complications and diseases associated with having high blood pressure. The truth of the matter is this trend is quite unsurprising. With the fashion in which we are eating nowadays, it is easy to see why high blood pressure is a problem.

Considering the current eating trends around the world, it is inevitable that health has suffered. We all eat too much of the wrong things. The fast-food culture is proving to be surprisingly strong. Many of us prefer to eat junk food because it is convenient and easily available. Children are growing obese and adults are growing unhealthy. Our current culture makes it difficult for us to make healthy choices. The current lifestyle choices of modern man are often very unhealthy.

Furthermore, it gets even more confusing for people nowadays because there are so many fly by night diet trends and diet rules. It gets difficult to figure out which diets are truly beneficial to your health and which ones are just a passing fad.

There are an abundance of different kinds of diets to choose from, it gets difficult to pick which one will be right for you.

Many people are concerned about their appearance but are not truly concerned about their health. In effect, you have teenagers who choose to starve themselves in order to look like the people they see on magazines. Health is more than just about having a nice body. It means having a body which functions properly.

High blood pressure is a serious problem. It prevents your body from functioning properly, and it might also lead to the development of other diseases. The number of people who are suffering from high blood pressure is growing by the day and it's surprising that we aren't taking this problem as seriously as we should. Many are already suffering and many more will suffer if the proper steps are not taken.

If you know that you have high blood pressure, don't ignore it! It can lead to serious complications which could possibly damage your health and your body permanently. If you don't get the proper medical attention that you need, you might end up with very serious problems.

The good news is that there is no reason for you to panic. You can easily take control of the situation if you can make a commitment to a healthier lifestyle.

Why Does Cholesterol Matter?

For the past few decades or so, cholesterol was always seen as the enemy. It was seen as the reason for heart failures and it was blamed for many things. People feared cholesterol, and the rule in every household was to keep it as low as possible.

While there are certain studies which now claim that cholesterol should not be demonized, it should still be monitored well to ensure that a person's body will continue to function well.

Here's a little surprise, you actually need cholesterol in your body. It is essential to life and is needed by cell membranes.

It is classified as a lipid and it is found in most animals. Even though it is a fat, it is essential to certain metabolic processes. In fact, most of our cholesterol is produced by the liver and most of the cells in our bodies. It helps in many biological processes like the absorption of vitamin D.

Cholesterol is useful but it has to be controlled. Health experts recommend that cholesterol should not exceed 5.5 mmol per liter. Those with pre-existing risk factors should aim for lower cholesterol. Unfortunately, a huge number of us ignore these numbers and recommendations. Most of us have a high cholesterol count.

If a person has too much cholesterol circulating in his or her bloodstream, it can get quite dangerous. Too much cholesterol can cause blood vessels to narrow, and eventually, be blocked. When blood vessels are blocked, it can lead to many different diseases like stroke or various heart diseases.

There are many factors which affect a person's cholesterol levels. Some people are more likely to have high-blood pressure because of genetics and family background. Others may have it because of a related medical condition like an under active thyroid gland, overconsumption of alcohol and obesity. Some risk factors are more dangerous than others and should be taken in to account.

It is important to look at a person's overall lifestyle in order to figure out the best possible solution to the problem.

Perhaps the most noticeable and controllable factor in preventing high blood pressure is monitoring a person's diet. While people's bodies might react differently even if they eat the same thing, switching to more health-conscious food choices will very likely improve a person's health conditions. Generally speaking, those who eat foods that are low in saturated fat can really help improve a person's overall health.

The majority of those who have high blood pressure do not show the symptoms of the condition. People over twenty years of age should ideally have their blood pressure checked at least once every year to ensure that they are in good condition.

They should even take the tests more often if they are in the high risk group. Consult your doctor or health care provider to find out how often you should take the test.

CHAPTER 3

MAJOR BENEFITS OF THE TLC DIET

Are you starting to think the TLC diet is for you? Well if so then take a look at the major benefits if you decide to follow this way of eating …

1. Easy to Follow

The diet is simple and easy to follow   There are no special kinds of foods that you need to cook. There is no need to learn a new recipe. You don't need to buy special and expensive ingredients. The diet is simple, straightforward and inexpensive.

The meals are easy to prepare. Since you don't need to strictly follow a specific meal plan, you have the freedom to modify the recipes per what is available for you.

Since this diet will allow you to modify your meals, it is also possible to adjust it if you are vegetarian or if you want it to be gluten-free. The important thing is to learn how to eat generally within the guidelines of the diet. Once you know and understand the basic principles which make the diet so effective, it will undoubtedly be much easier for you to modify the diet in accordance with your individual needs.

2. It is Proven Effective

The diet is healthy and proven effective   The effects of the TLC diet are long-term. This is because rather than providing a quick- fix solution to the problem, the TLC diet encourages positive

changes in a person's lifestyle. The true secret of maintaining a healthy lifestyle is knowing how to keep eating healthy and how to continue exercising for a long time. Rather than a race, think of health as a marathon. It cannot be rushed and it must be taken slowly but surely.

3. Educates People

The TLC diet actually educates people.   With   the   TLC diet, a person is made aware of what he or she should eat and drink. A person learns how to choose what is healthy. This means knowing how to shop for healthy items, how to read labels and how to prepare meals in a healthy way. A person will also know how to compute how much saturated fat he or she is recommended to consume. Unlike some other diets, you will not be told what you should eat in every single meal. Therefore, it is up to a person to choose his or her meals according to what he or she learns.

Well those are just a few of the main benefits gained by following the principles of the TLC Diet.

In the next part we will look more specifically at what to eat and how to get your proper nutrients in.

CHAPTER 4

TLC NUTRITION OVERVIEW - GETTING YOUR NUTRIENTS & WHAT TO EAT

To lower your cholesterol levels, there's no getting around the fact that you must do something about the food you eat.

The TLC program's major focus is to create a nutritious way of eating that will provide the correct nutrients and will reduce the amount of saturated fat you eat.

These Saturated fats are the fats that elevate your cholesterol levels. First you want to reduce the foods high in saturated fats, like fatty cuts of meat and whole milk products you eat.

You will also have to replace some of the animal fats and choose some healthy, monounsaturated oils – olive oil, for example.

Another good option is choosing a fatty acid supplement like Omega-3. These fats will keep the good cholesterol up and lower the bad one.

The types of food you eat can be as important as their calorie content. What is good for one person may not be the same for the other. It is thus important to understand your metabolic system and nutritional needs.

What are calories? There is so much hype surrounding calories these days. All of us know that in order to lose weight, we must burn calories. But what exactly are calories? In simple words, calories are units of energy in food or drinks required by the body to perform its functions. The amount of calories needed by your body depends on the amount of energy required by your body to keep warm.

This is exactly what your body needs, irrespective of your activities. Typically, the larger an individual, the greater their caloric need is or their basal metabolic rate – which is the amount of energy expended by a body at rest. The basal metabolic rate remains the same daily.

If your body needs, in example, 2,000 calories today, it will require the same amount tomorrow and the next day and so on. Basal metabolic rate varies from person to person, depending on the body size and amount of work you do.

What Can You Eat?

The TLC program is based on consuming a wide array of different foods but in doing so, getting a proper ratio of nutrients to fuel your body effectively. Food choices are not restricted per se, but must be consumed in a limited amount. These amounts are sometimes a percentage of your total calorie intake for each day.

- Saturated fat Less than 7 % of total calories
- Polyunsaturated fat Up to 10 % of total calories
- Monounsaturated fat Up to 20 % of total calories
- Carbohydrate 50 % to 60 % of total calories
- Soluble fiber At least 5 to 10 grams a day
- Protein Approximately 15 % of total calories

Fat

The biggest part of TLC diet program is about fats and is where we are going to focus our attention on in this beginners guide. If you get the correct amount of good fats in your diet most things will fall into place (Carbs, Protein & Fiber).

These fats can help you fight those cholesterol levels, or help you feed them. You have to learn what fat actually is in order to defeat it – get to know your enemy before fighting it!

Fat seems to be a dreaded word for most of us. But have you ever wondered why there is so much hue and cry about fat? First, I need you to understand this.

Dietary fat is different than your body fat.

It appears that the lack of knowledge of nutrition scares most to think dietary fat is bad. It can be considered word and image association where you hear the word "fat" and automatically associate it with the fat on your belly. Automatically you think, "Uh oh, I don't want any more fat on my stomach, I don't want that food if it has fat." So, is a low-fat diet a solution for all ills?

Well, before answering this question, it is important to find whether you are eating healthy fats or not. Healthy fats include seeds, nuts, and unrefined oils and naturally occurring fats in vegetables and meats. The key lies in maintaining moderation and optimizing nutritional benefits. Experts recommend that fats and oil should suffice for at least 10–40 percent of your regular energy needs.

Though fats have earned a poor reputation fortheir effect on heart health and obesity, some fat is ESSENTIAL for health and wellbeing.

Fats help in the absorption of carotenoids and fat-soluble vitamins - A, D, E, K Supply essential fatty acids needed by the body, which it cannot make on its own, such as omega-3 – which is an unsaturated fat that we must consume from our diets mainly found in fish. Fats have the potential to harm as well as help our health; depending on their fatty acid composition, their nutritional value, and their condition.

When used in a natural, unadulterated state, fat offers optimal nutritional benefits. On the other hand, a very-low- fat diet can compromise our health and ability to lose weight.

Fatty Acids

When you eat food, the fat comprised in the food is known as fatty acids. Typically considered "good fats," fatty acids are known as the building blocks of many cellular structures and hormonal patterns in the human body.

Healthy Nuts, Seeds, Fats And Oils.

Healthy Nuts & Seeds To Consume: Almonds, Pistachios, Walnuts, Hazelnuts, Sesame Seeds Pecans, Brazil Nuts, Sunflower Seeds, Macadamia Nuts, Cashews, Peanuts, Pumpkin Seeds, Chia Seeds.

Fats and oils to use: Almond Oil, Red Palm Oil, Extra Virgin Olive Oil, Grape seed oil, Sesame Oil, Flax Seed Oil, Macadamia Nut Oil Hemp, Coconut Oil, Safflower Oil.

These fatty acids help in the transfer of oxygen to different parts of the body through the bloodstream. These fats help keep skin healthy, thus preventing signs of early aging. These promote cell membrane development and are essential for strong organs and tissue.

They help the body process cholesterol and rid the arteries of plaque or cholesterol build-up. Fatty acids boost the functioning of adrenal and thyroid glands, thus helping regulate weight.

CHAPTER 5

COOKING THE TLC WAY – SAMPLE MEAL OPTIONS

In this section, I'm going to introduce you to some delicious TLC recipes.

Breakfast Smoothie

Ingredients:

1 cup of fresh blueberries

½ cup of chopped baby spinach 1 cup of avocado, chopped

2 tbsp of almonds, minced 1 cup of coconut milk

½ cup of ice cubes (optional)

Preparation: Wash and drain the baby spinach. Combine with other ingredients in a blender and mix for about 30 seconds. Serve cold.

Fruit Salad

Ingredients:

1 cup of berries

½ cup of pineapple cubes

½ cup of chopped apple 5 mint springs

1 tbsp of fresh lime juice

1 tsp of lime zest ¼ cup of water 1 tsp of cinnamon

1 tsp of agave syrup

Preparation: In a small saucepan combine ¼ cup of water, mint spring, fresh lime juice and lime zest. Allow it to boil over medium temperature and cook for about 2-3 minutes. Remove from the heat and cool. Meanwhile, in a large bowl, combine 1 cup of berries, ½ cup of pineapple cubes and ½ cup of chopped apple. Add agave syrup and mix well. Pour the lime mixture over the salad and let it stand in the refrigerator for 20-30 minutes.

Remove from the refrigerator and sprinkle with 1 tsp of cinnamon before serving.

Grilled Eggplant Slices With Chopped Fennel

Ingredients:

1 large eggplant

½ cup of chopped fennel 1 tbsp of olive oil

1 tsp of chopped parsley

Preparation: Peel the eggplant and cut into 3 equal slices. Bake it in a barbecue pan without oil. When done, spread olive oil over it, sprinkle with fennel and parsley. (These eggplant slices are great cold, so you can leave them overnight in a refrigerator)

Turkey Fillet With Walnuts And Maple Syrup

Ingredients:

3 turkey fillets

½ cup of walnuts

1 tsp of maple syrup

¼ cup of water

1 tbsp of olive oil salt to taste

Preparation: Fry the fillets in a barbecue pan, over a low temperature, for about 15 minutes, or until tender. Remove the pan from the heat and add water, maple syrup and walnuts. Mix well and fry for another 5-6 minutes until the water evaporates. Stir constantly. Allow it to cool for a while before serving.

Beef Chop With Pineapple And Tumeric

Ingredients:

1.5 pounds of beef chop, boneless 2 tbsp of coconut oil

1 tbsp of olive oil

½ cup of coconut milk 1 tsp of tumeric

¼ tsp of pepper

1 medium pineapple, peeled and chopped

Preparation: Wash and dry the meat. Cut into bite size cubes. Combine the meat with coconut oil, coconut milk, tumeric, pepper and pineapple. Mix well and set side for 15 minutes. Use a large wok pan to heat up the olive oil. Remove te meat and pineapple chops from the marinade and fry for about 5-7 minutes on each side. Now pour in the remaining marinade, cover the wok pan and cook for 30 minutes over a medium temperature. The marinade will become thick and the meat soft. Remove from the heat and serve.

Salmon With Zucchini

Ingredients:

1 pound of sliced salmon fillets 2 small zucchinis

6 Brussels sprouts

3 tbsp of extra virgin olive oil

¼ tsp of pepper

Preparation: Peel and slice zucchinis into 0.5 inch thick circle shape slices. Cut salmon fillets into bite size pieces. Heat up one tbsp of olive oil in a large skillet and add your salmon fillets. Fry them up for about 10 minutes, or until they are nice and crispy. When done, move them to a plate covered with a kitchen paper to soak up the grease. Set aside.

Cut the Brussels sprouts in half. Combine with zucchini slices in a large bowl and add 2 tbsp of the remaining olive oil. Move the vegetables to the skillet and cook until the Brussel sprouts are tender. This should take no more than 10 minutes. Add your salmon fillets to the skillet, cover and allow it to rewarm. Serve and enjoy.

CHAPTER 6

SMART CHOICES, EATING OUT AND SOCIAL EVENTS ON THE TLC DIET

During the first couple of days of your TLC diet, you may be under the impression that it is difficult to follow. However, if you stick at it for longer than a fortnight, it'll become easier and easier for you to follow, eventually becoming a habit.

As we mentioned earlier in the book, there may be times when you're too busy, or you may be going out with friends to a restaurant. During this time, you may be tempted to let the diet go.

The key to sticking with the diet is to prepare yourself for every possible situation you can think of. It is important that you try to make sure you always have access to health food, regardless. As long as you have healthy foods available at all times, you will be able to eat healthy.

This means you should take part in smart shopping, know how to cook your food and you should know exactly what to eat when you're eating out and attending social events.

Once you are able to handle all of that, it will be easy for you to eat healthily, regardless of where you may be. You're not going to have any excuses to run to the nearest fast food chain or eat chocolate.

The way you cook is a big influence on how healthy your food is going to be. The right cooking technique can make a health ingredient even healthier. On another note, the wrong technique can make things a lot worse. Take deep frying as an example – you're taking a vegetable and turning it into a giant sponge of fat. If you want to stay healthy, then you need to learn healthy cooking techniques.

Cooking Techniques

Cook using low-fat methods. Avoid using too much butter and oil. There are certain techniques that are preferred by advocates of the TLC diet.

These cooking techniques include:

- Grilling
- Steaming
- Boiling
- Roasting
- Baking
- Poaching

It is okay to sauté or even do some light frying, but keep your use of oil and butter low. You may want to invest in a good non- stick pan that will allow you to cook without using butter.

Eating Out On The TLC Diet

What you choose to eat during your outing all depends on the type of restaurant you choose.

Here, I am going to list Chinese restaurants and Italian as those seem to be pretty popular.

If you chose to eat out at a Chinese restaurant, stay away from the fried rice and go for food that doesn't contain MSG. Chinese cuisine consists of a lot of vegetables, but many times, their cooking styles are no good. Thankfully, on the menu, you'll be able to find barbecues, roasted and steamed food.

If you chose to eat out at an Italian restaurant, don't eat too much bread. When you choose bread as a side dish, it can be easy to overindulge. Eating too much, however, can do more harm than good. If you chose pizza, go for ones that are packed full of vegetable toppings and choose half the amount of cheese. Sometimes, these restaurants overload pizza with processed meat like pepperoni, bacon and sausage.

If you're going for pasta, choose the red sauce because this is healthier than any cream.

CHAPTER 7

GETTING PHYSICALLY ACTIVE

I'm going to tell you right now, if you want to be healthy, you need to get out there and get physical.

Regardless of your age, it's never too late for you to start exercising, so don't ever use your age as an excuse – there's 70 year old's out there doing extraordinary things with a bit of fitness!

In fact, the older you are, the more you should exercise. No, I'm not joking. Unless your doctor has advised against it, there's no reason not to. Exercise isn't going to have a negative impact on your body. Of course, before you get physically active, you should speak with your doctor to get the "go ahead," this way, you will feel better.

You just need to learn how to fight through that laziness for the sake of your own health and get your body to start moving. Trust us, even the smallest of changes in your lifestyle can lead to a huge change in your body, so don't hesitate to start a good exercise regimen and stick to it.

At first, you're not going to like exercise, but eventually, as it becomes a part of your lifestyle, you're going to enjoy it.

Types of Exercises:

- Walking

- Jogging

- Swimming

- Yoga

Those are only for types of exercise you can take part in. Honestly, you can easily create your own exercise routine that is fun for you.

Just look on youtube for at home exercise programs and you will find a multitude of fun and easy to perform programs.

CONCLUSION

Well we have reached the pinnacle of our beginners guide on the TLC Diet and I want to congratulate you for making it this far. In this final part we will be summarizing the main points we have covered so far and hopefully put to ease any questions or doubts you may have.

Tips To Start Today

At first, it's not going to be easy – no diet is easy, regardless of who you are, above all else however, the major thing to consider is sources of fat in your diet and monitoring saturated fat levels to lower your cholesterol.

While this seems difficult, after about a week or so, you'll start to pick up on the routine and before you know it, the TLC diet will naturally become a part of your lifestyle.

Here's a little bit of advice for you – put some time and effort into making your meals. You may even want to enroll in a nice yoga class (there may be one going on right now in your area). If you cannot find a yoga class, you can find many yoga videos online, which will allow you to practice yoga in the comfort of your own home.

Also, it may help if you have a nice support system going on. The more friends you have that will take part in this diet with you, the better off you're going to be.

In the end, don't let anything get in your way and remember the benefits of the TLC diet! You can also reward yourself. Rewarding yourself will give you something to look forward to. Just don't reward yourself with food – go for a new shirt or something along those lines.

Well that's it, you've reached the end. Wish you all the best in your journey to reduce your cholesterol levels by following the TLC diet.

Let Food Be Thy Medicine And Medicine Be Thy Food

Hippocrates

Printed by Libri Plureos GmbH in Hamburg,
Germany

9 786069 836934